You're my
Valentine

From: _______________

To: _______________

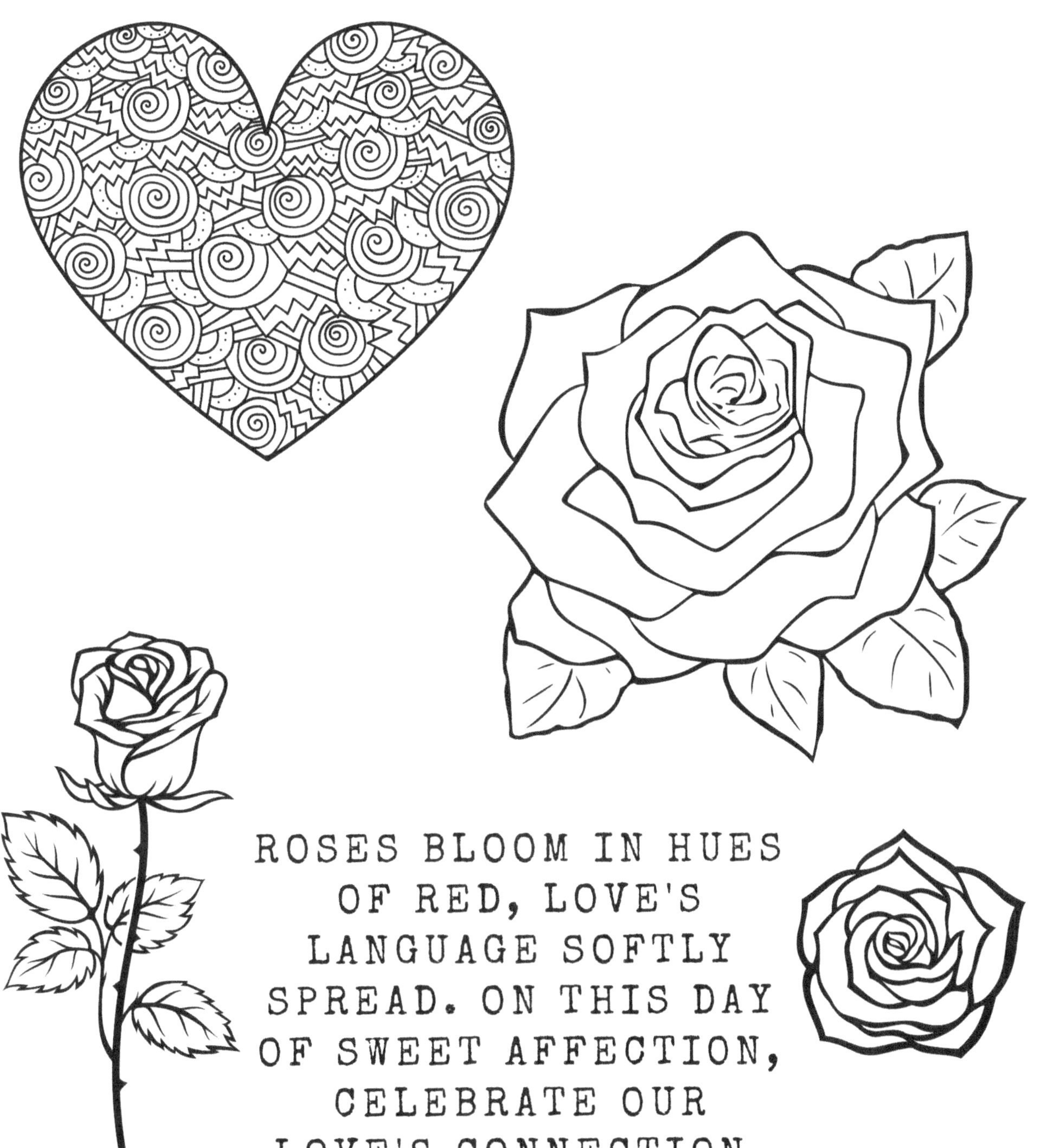


ROSES BLOOM IN HUES
OF RED, LOVE'S
LANGUAGE SOFTLY
SPREAD. ON THIS DAY
OF SWEET AFFECTION,
CELEBRATE OUR
LOVE'S CONNECTION.

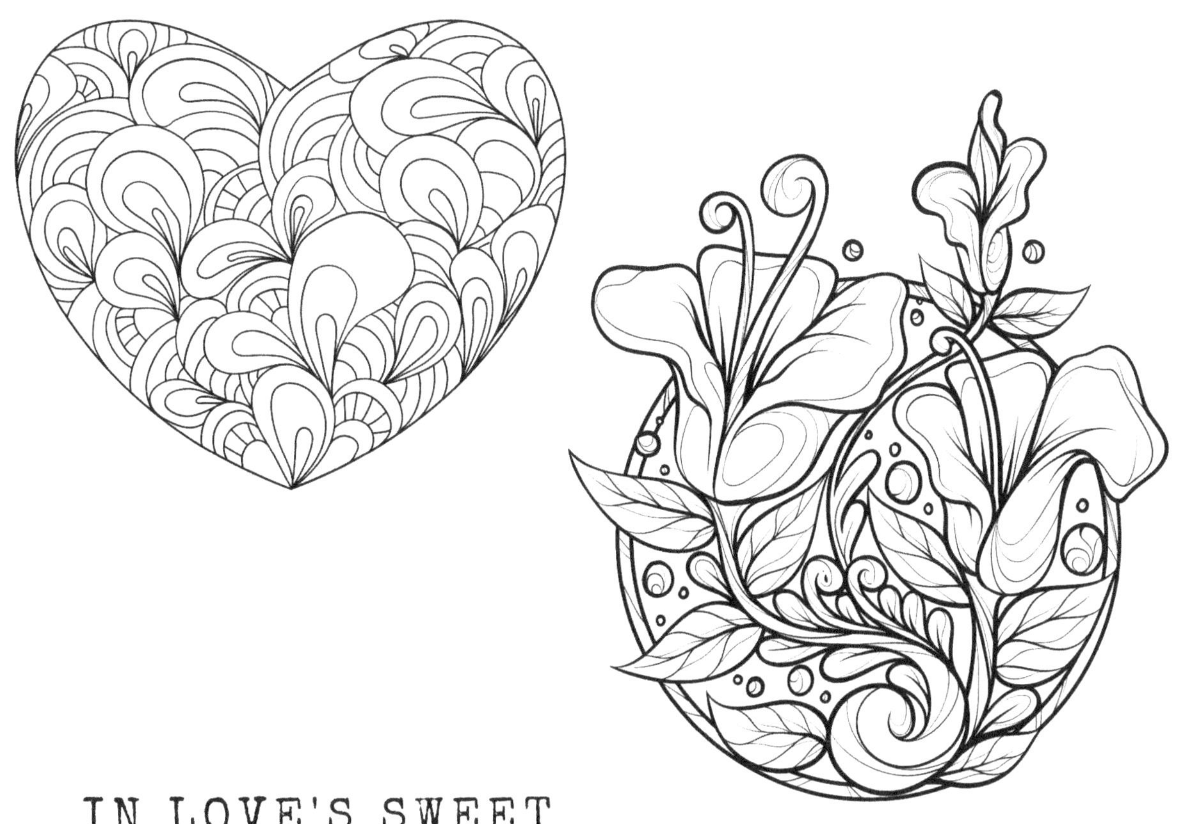

IN LOVE'S SWEET EMBRACE, HEARTS ENTWINE, A DANCE OF PASSION, YOURS AND MINE. VALENTINE'S WHISPERS, A TENDER RHYME, FOREVER BOUND, THROUGH ENDLESS TIME.

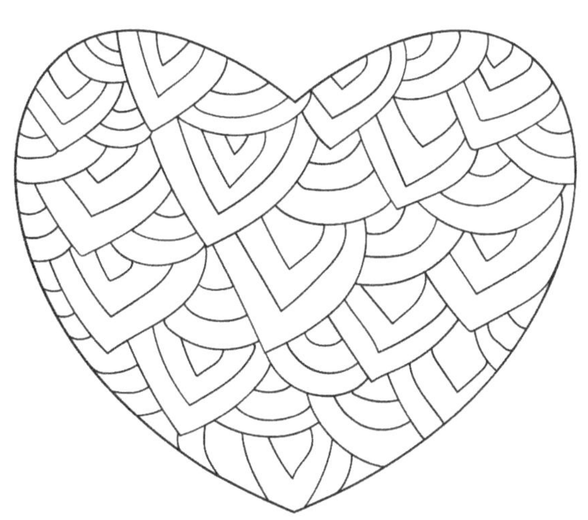

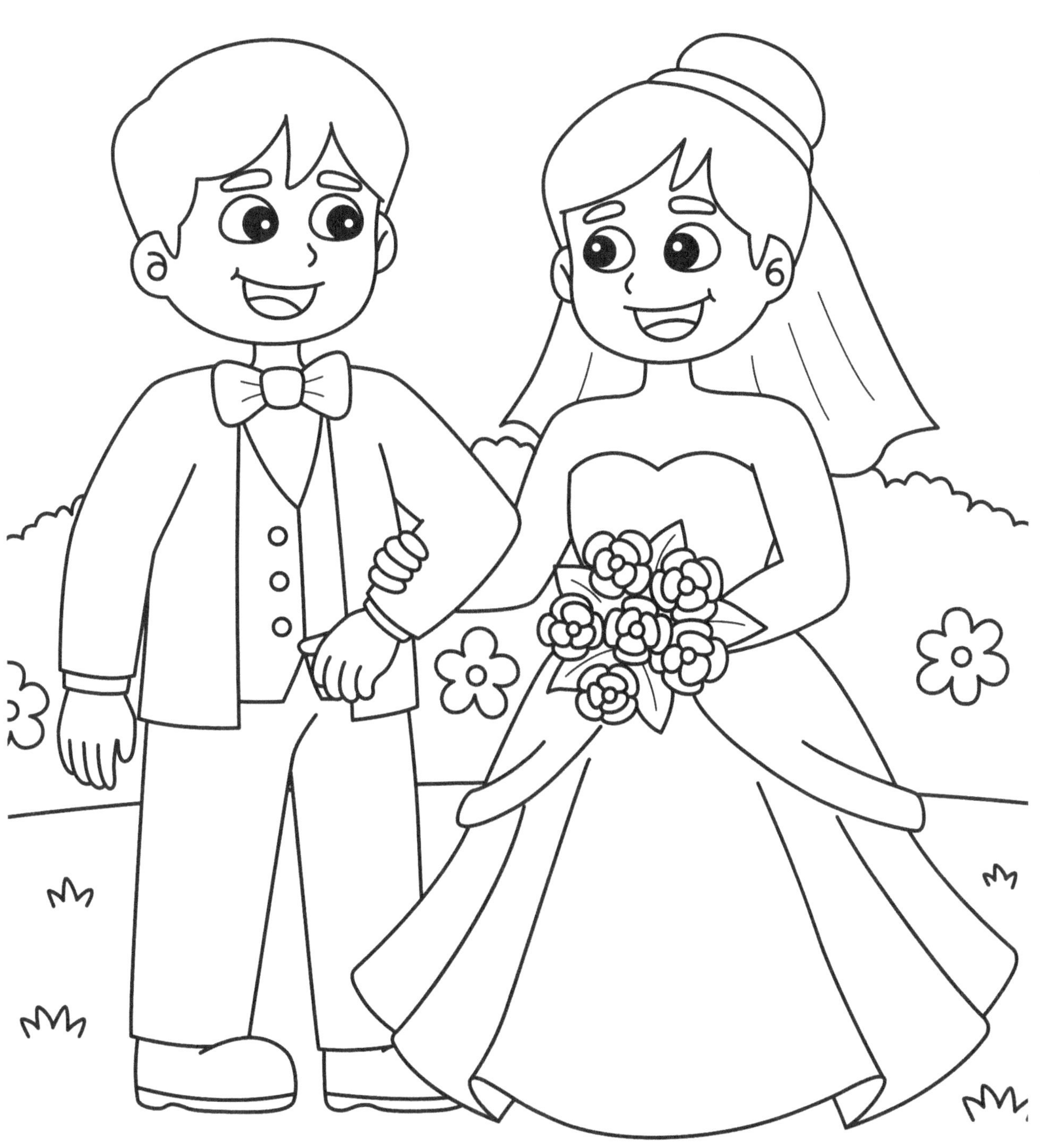

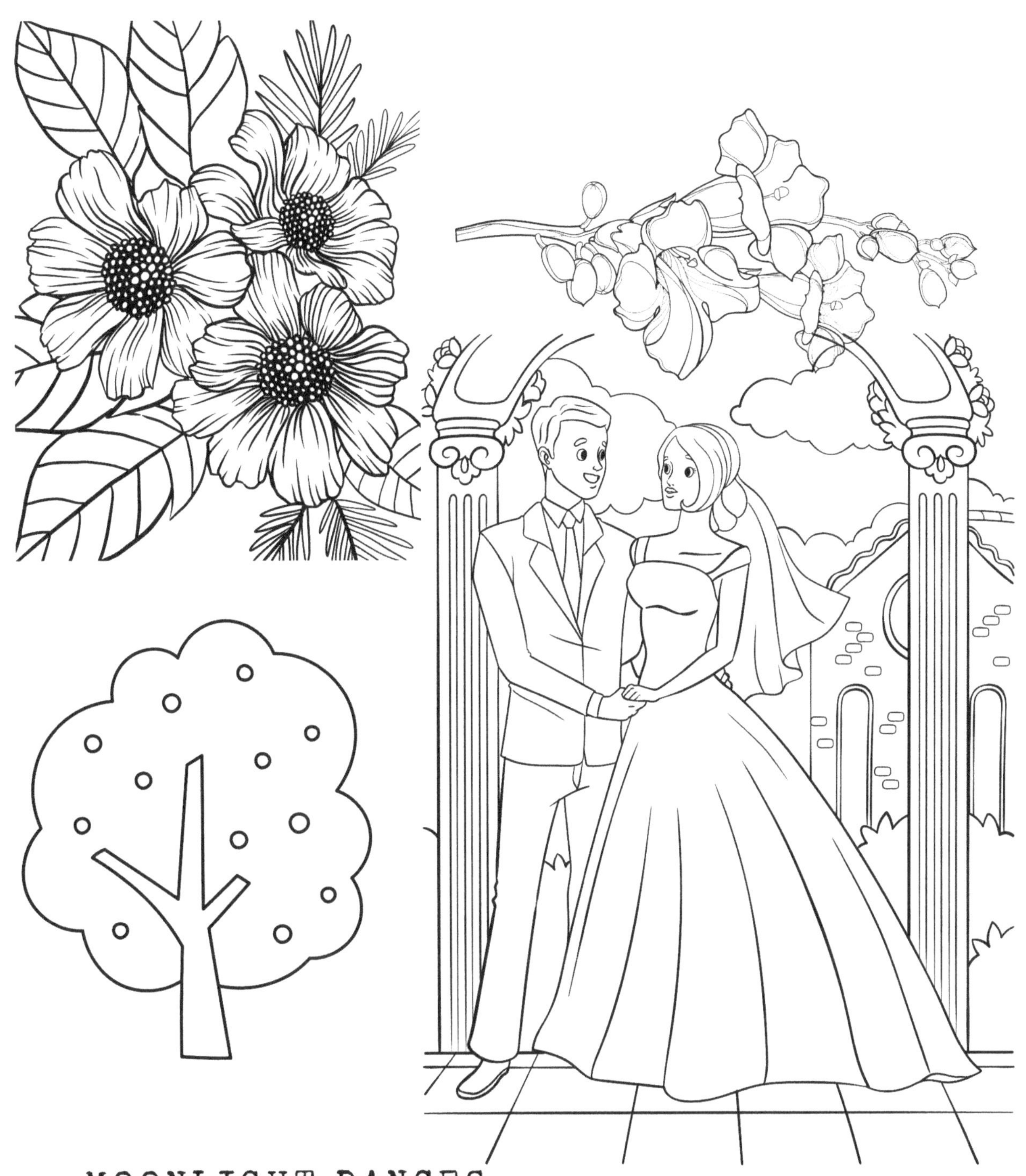

MOONLIGHT DANCES,
STARS ALIGN, OUR
LOVE STORY, PURE AND
DIVINE. HAPPY
VALENTINE'S, MY
DEAR, IN YOUR ARMS, I
HOLD LOVE NEAR.

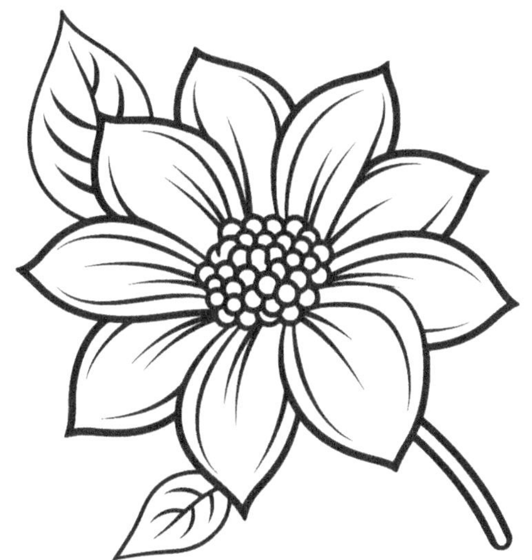

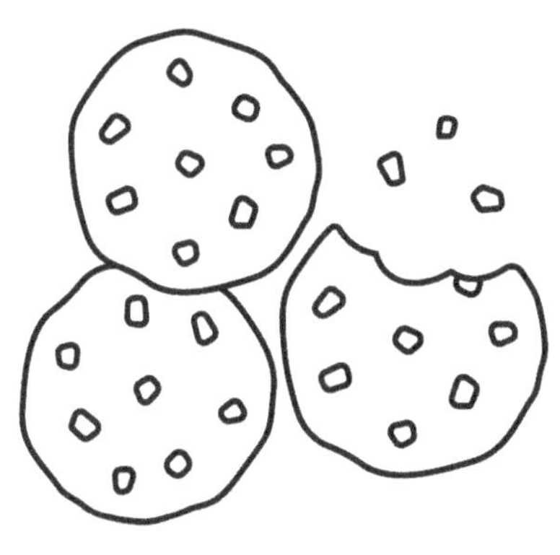

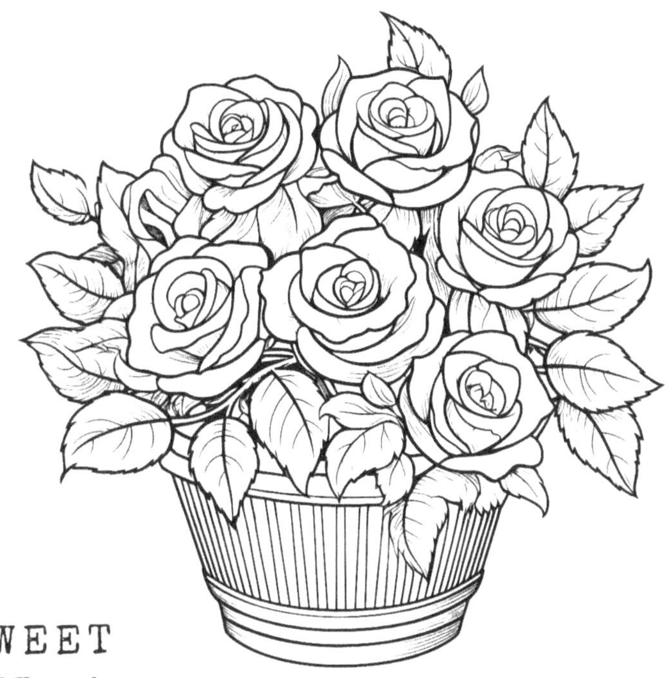

CHOCOLATES SWEET
AND ROSES FAIR, A
LOVE SO TRUE,
BEYOND COMPARE.
HAPPY VALENTINE'S,
FOREVERMORE, IN
YOUR LOVE, I DEEPLY
ADORE.

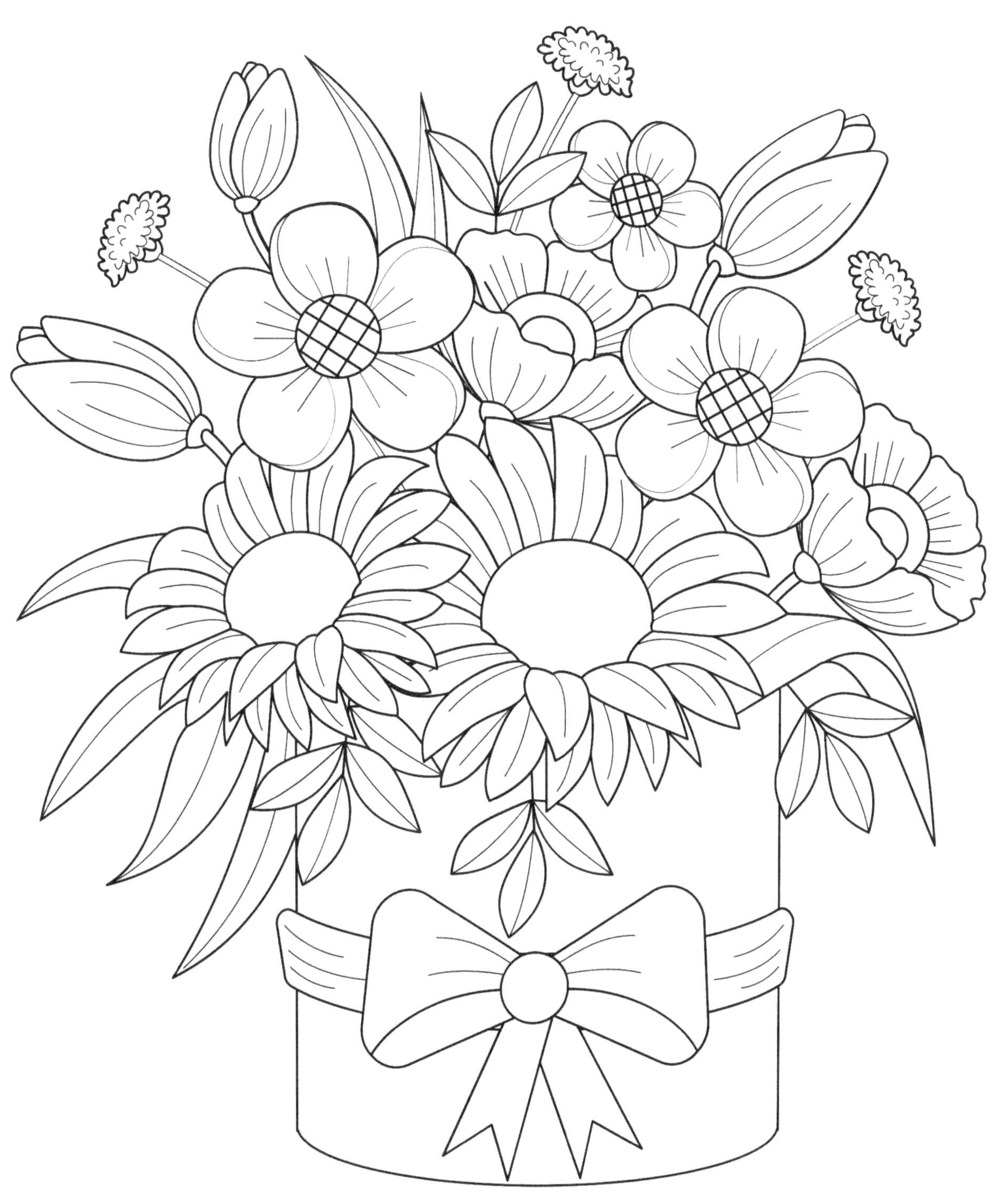

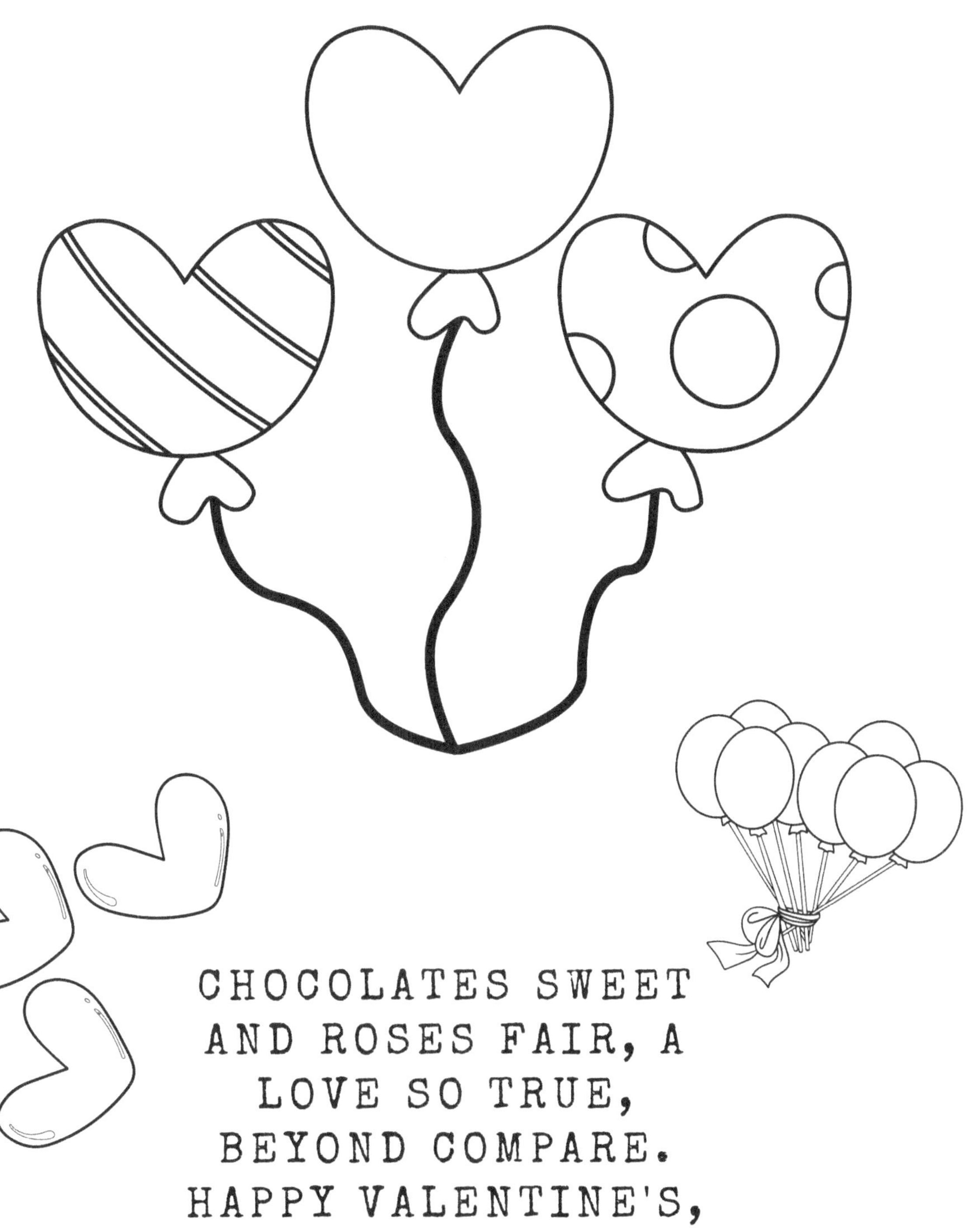

CHOCOLATES SWEET
AND ROSES FAIR, A
LOVE SO TRUE,
BEYOND COMPARE.
HAPPY VALENTINE'S,
FOREVERMORE, IN
YOUR LOVE, I DEEPLY
ADORE.

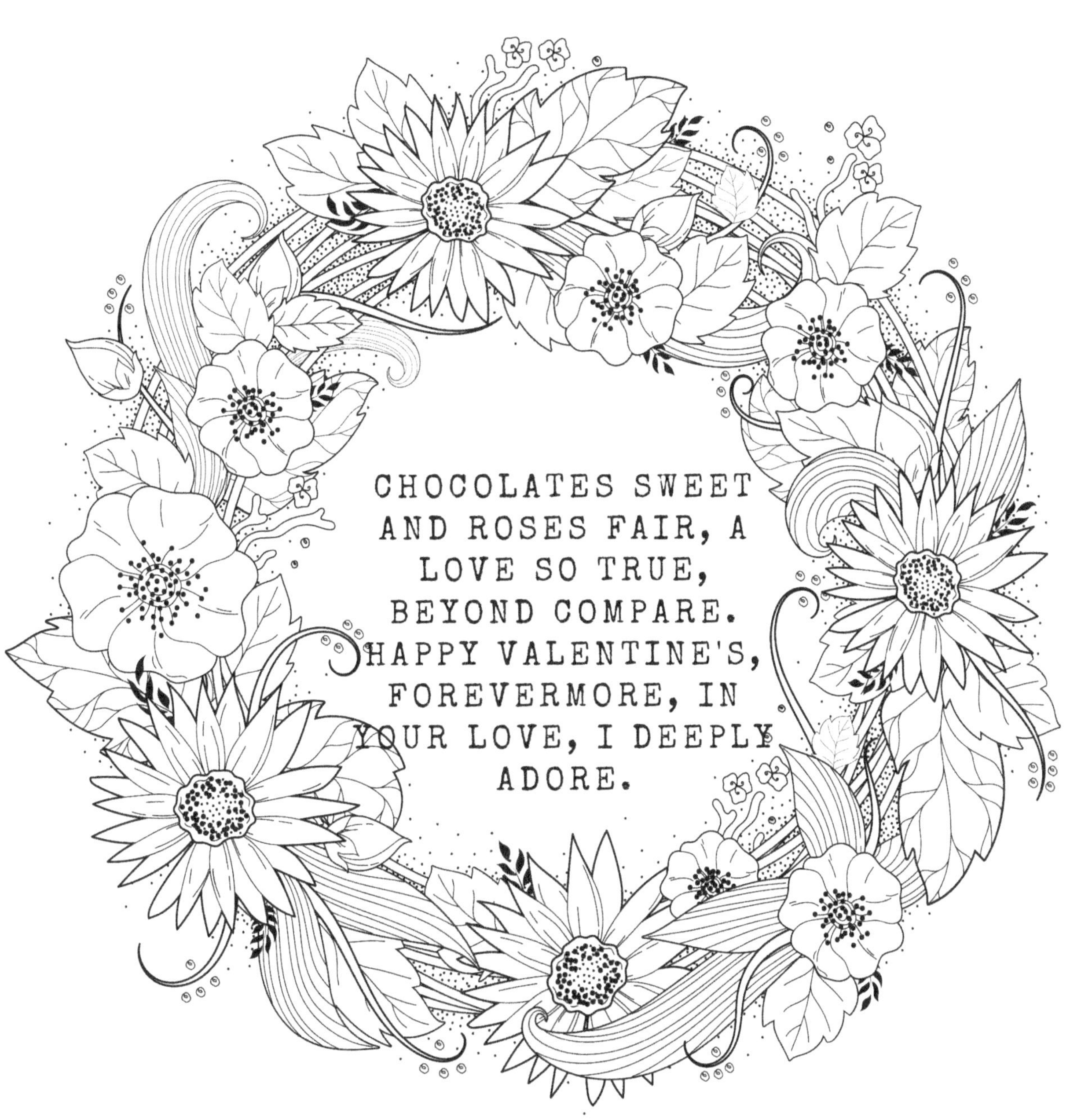
CHOCOLATES SWEET
AND ROSES FAIR, A
LOVE SO TRUE,
BEYOND COMPARE.
HAPPY VALENTINE'S,
FOREVERMORE, IN
YOUR LOVE, I DEEPLY
ADORE.

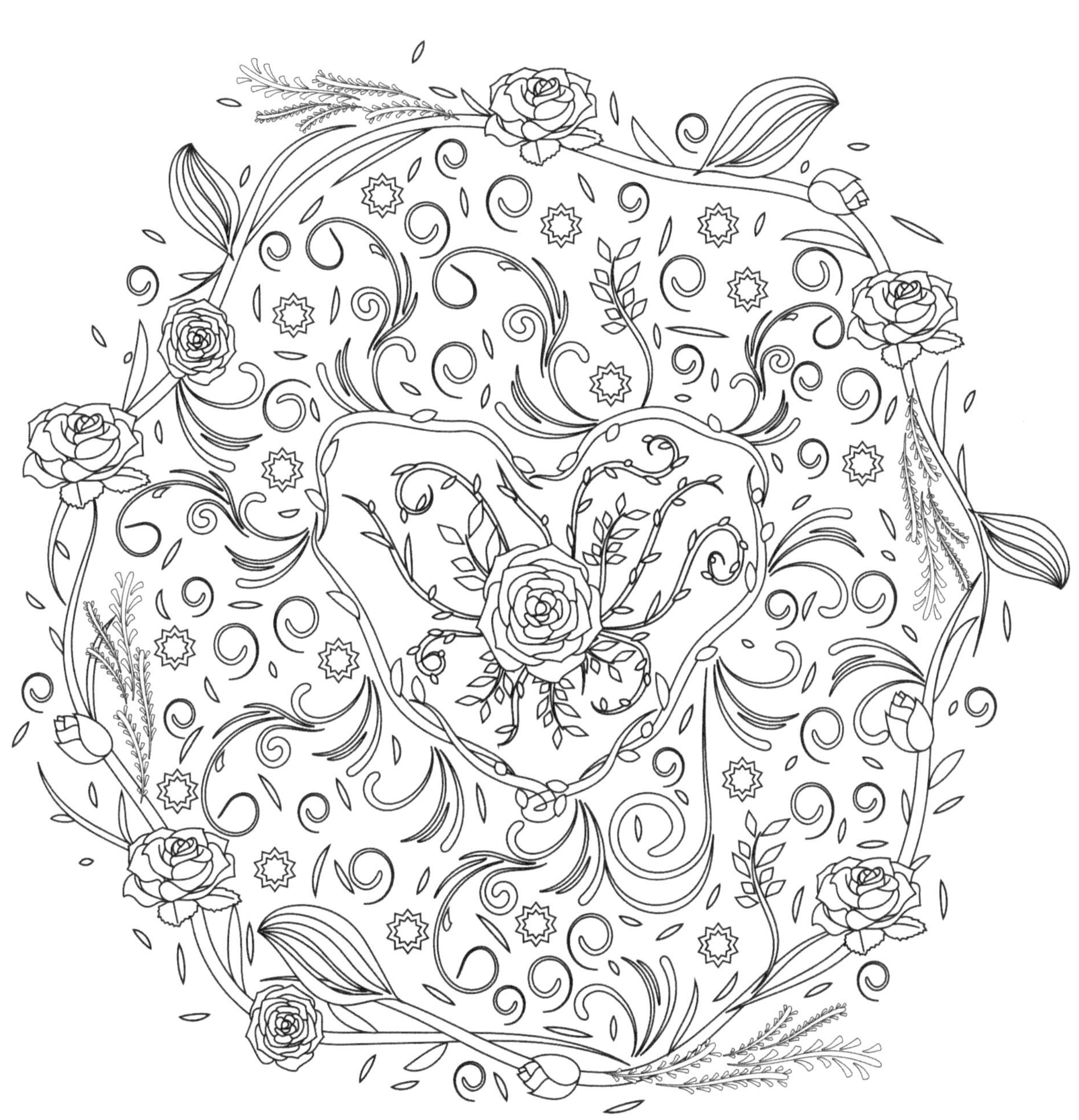

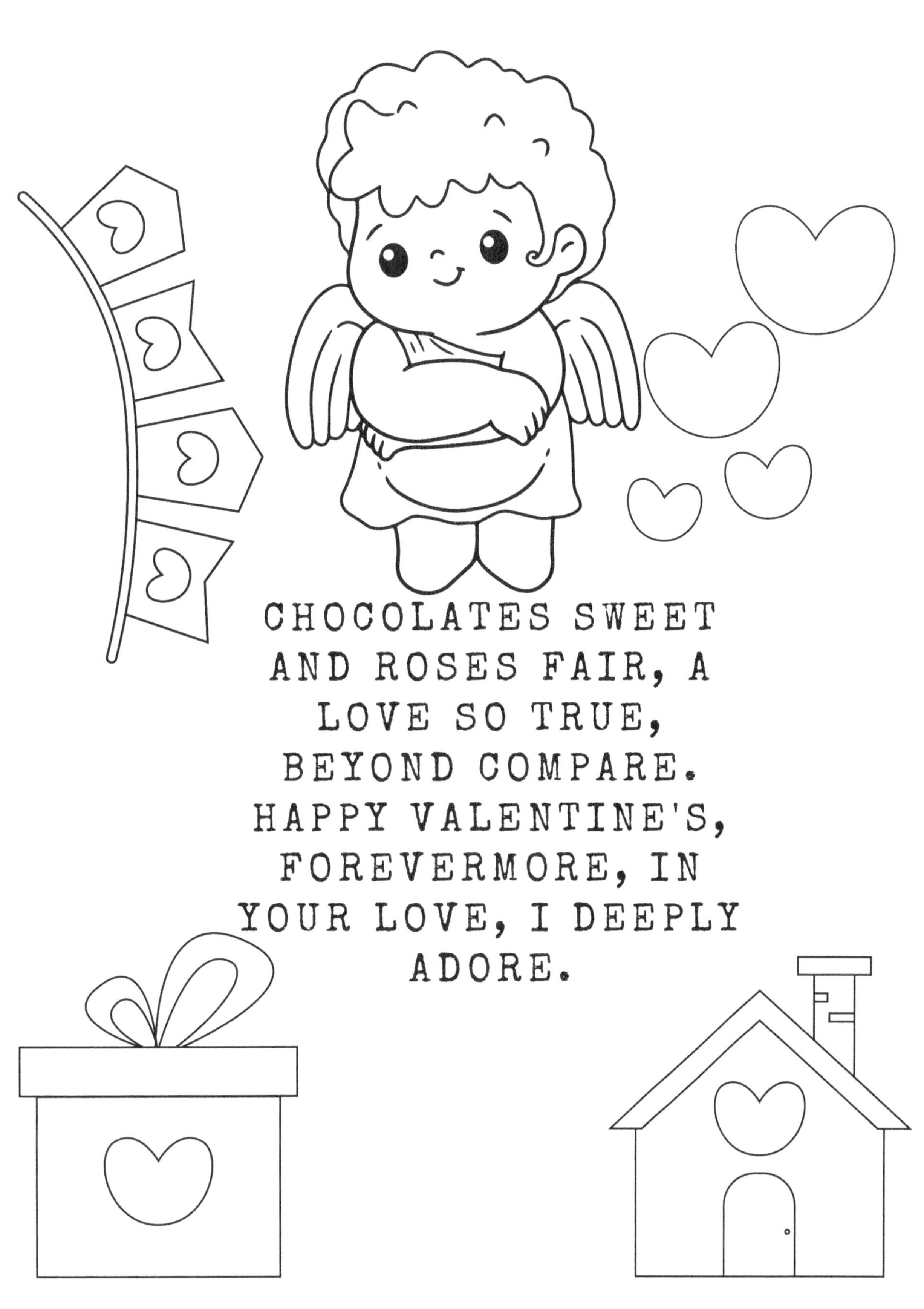
CHOCOLATES SWEET
AND ROSES FAIR, A
LOVE SO TRUE,
BEYOND COMPARE.
HAPPY VALENTINE'S,
FOREVERMORE, IN
YOUR LOVE, I DEEPLY
ADORE.

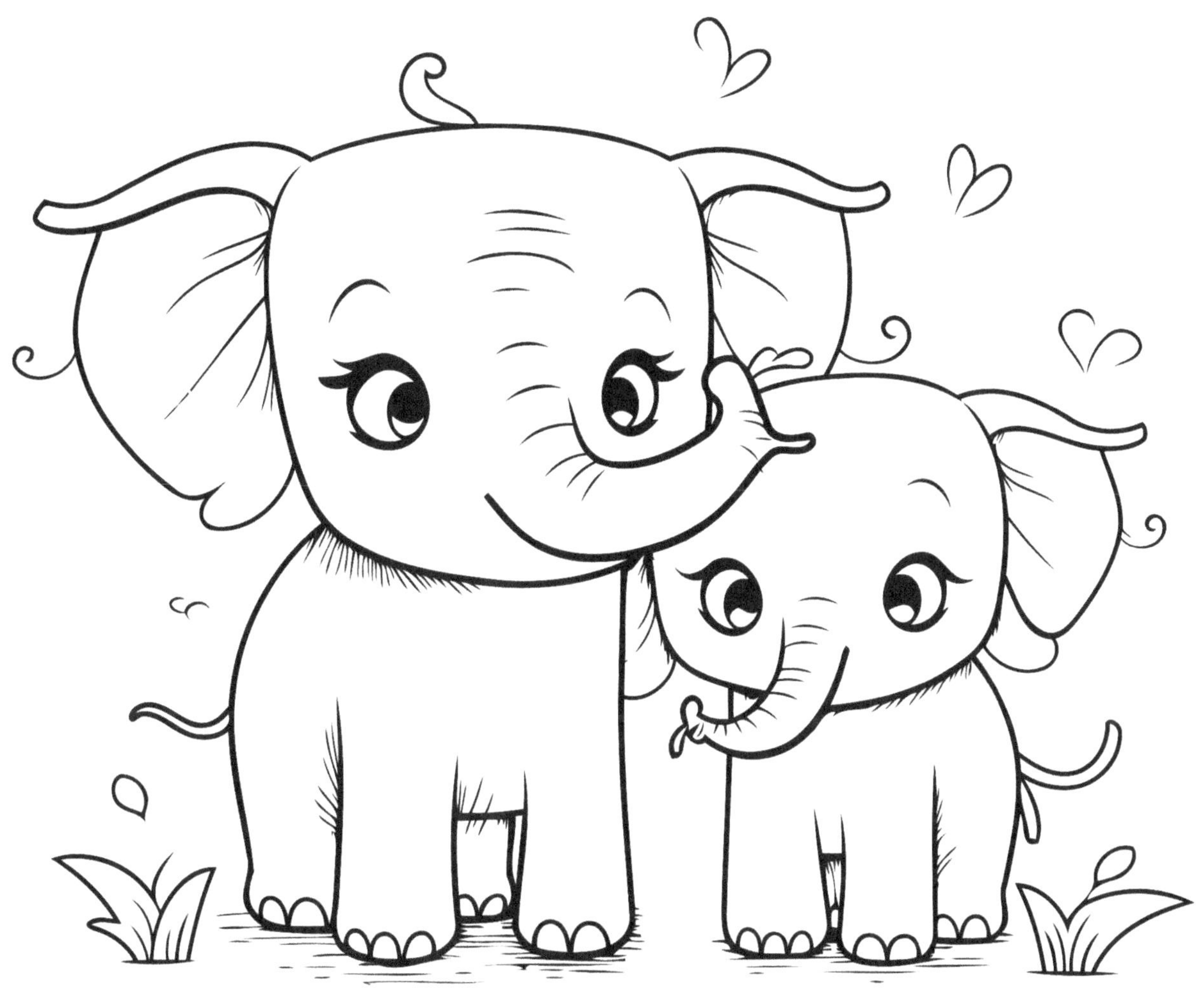

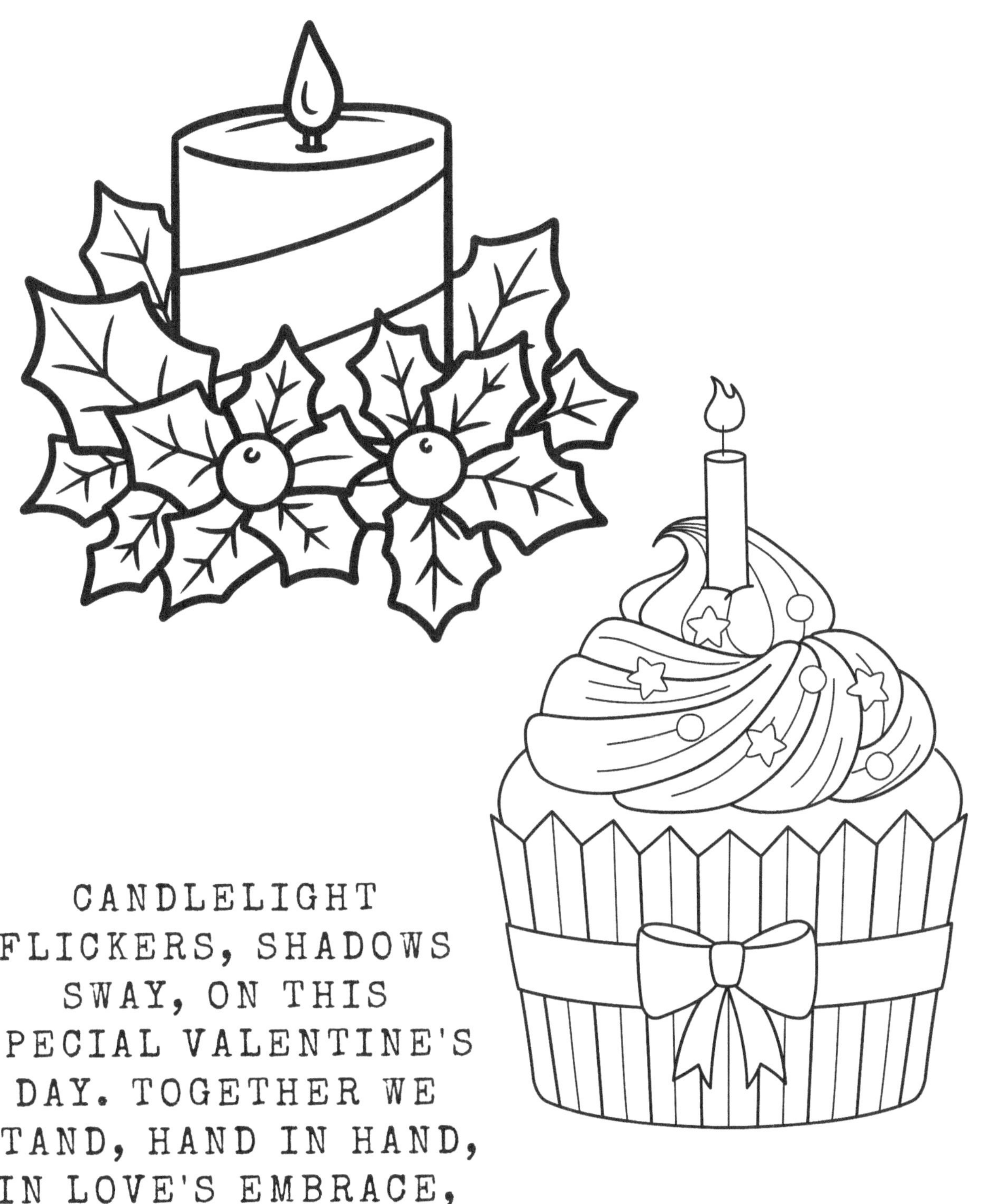

CANDLELIGHT
FLICKERS, SHADOWS
SWAY, ON THIS
SPECIAL VALENTINE'S
DAY. TOGETHER WE
STAND, HAND IN HAND,
IN LOVE'S EMBRACE,
FOREVER WE'LL LAND.

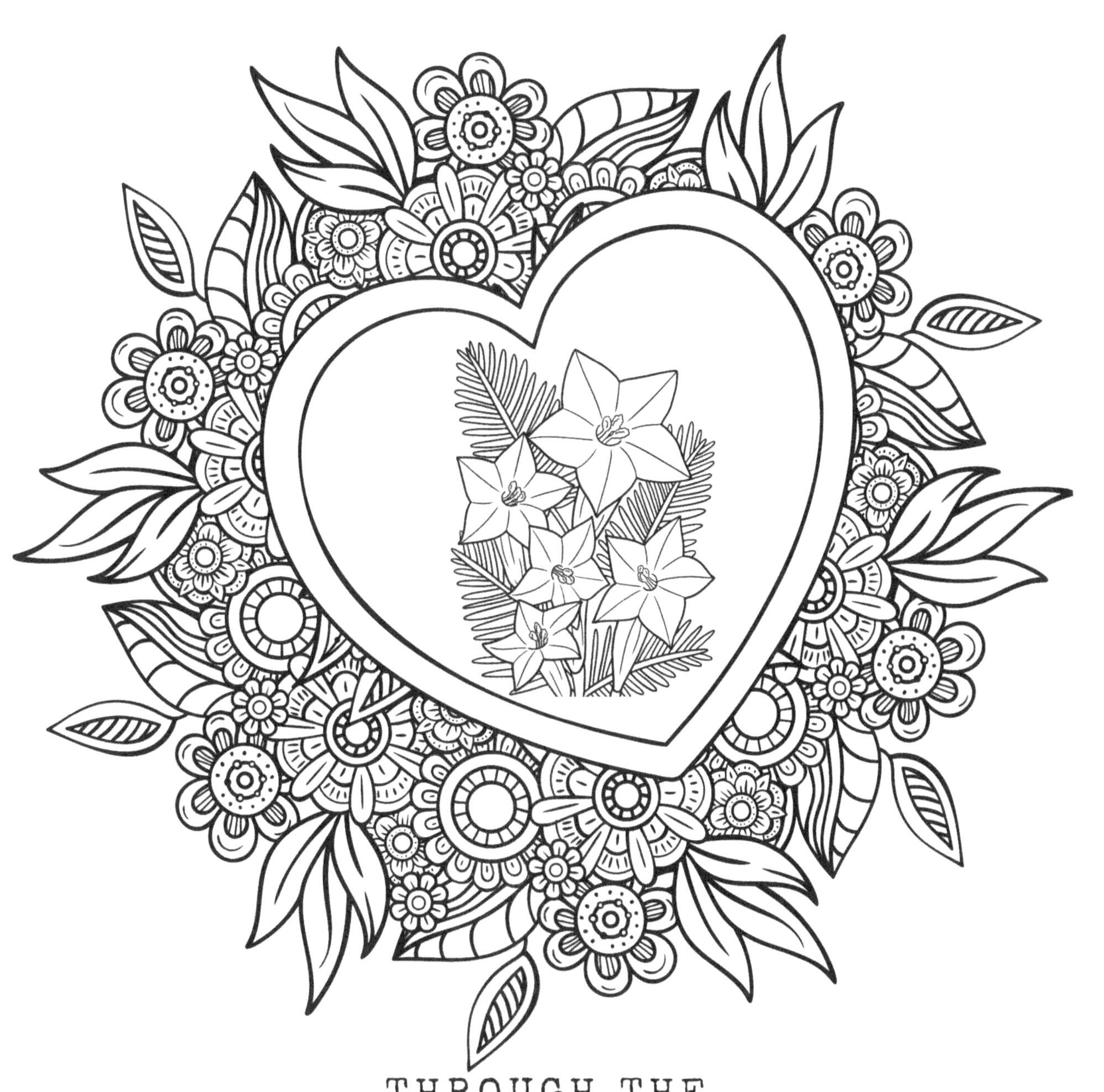

THROUGH THE
SEASONS, LOVE'S
EMBRACE,
VALENTINE'S CHARM, A
TIMELESS GRACE. IN
YOUR GAZE, A WORLD
UNFURLS, A LOVE
STORY THAT FOREVER
SWIRLS.

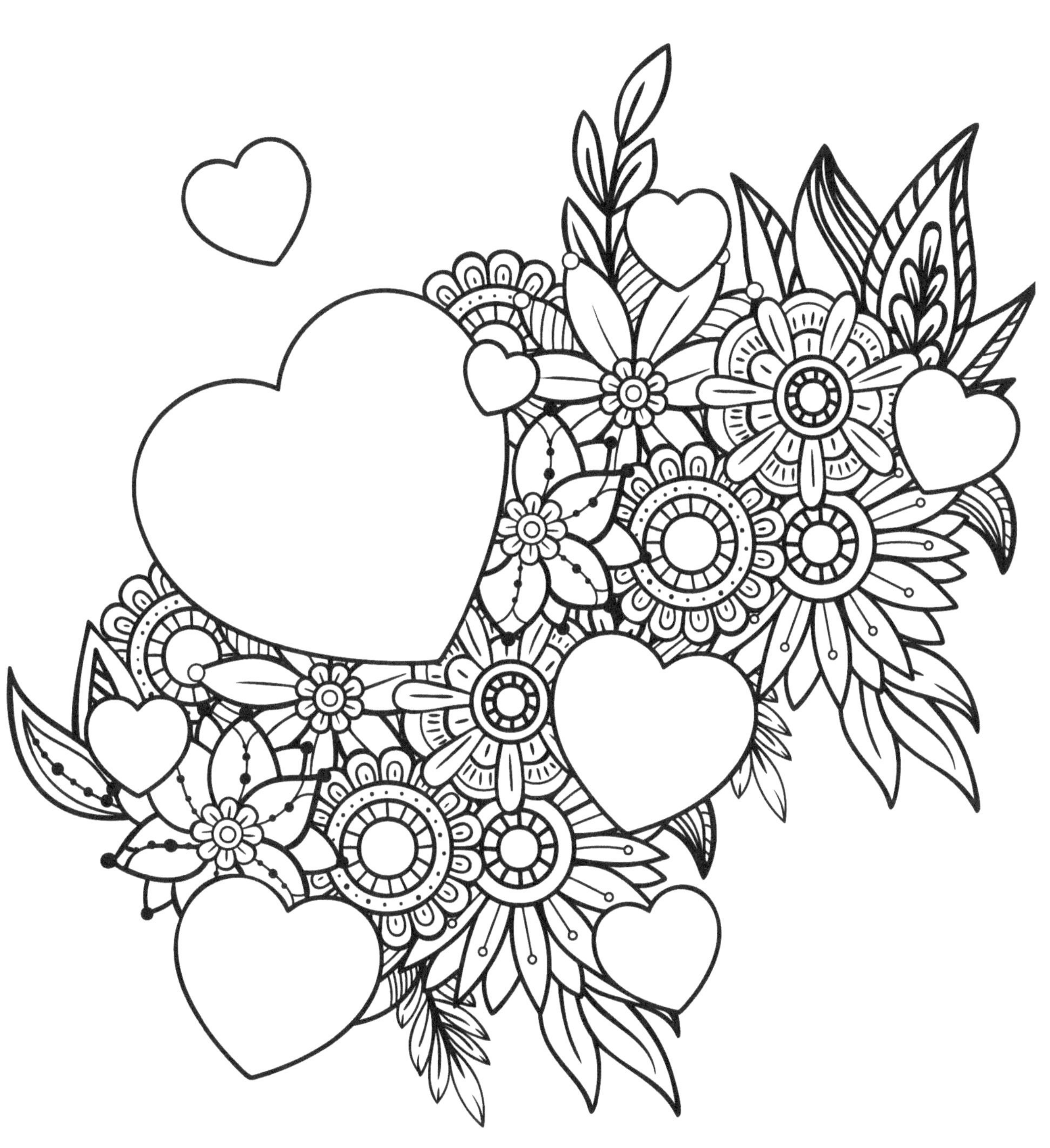

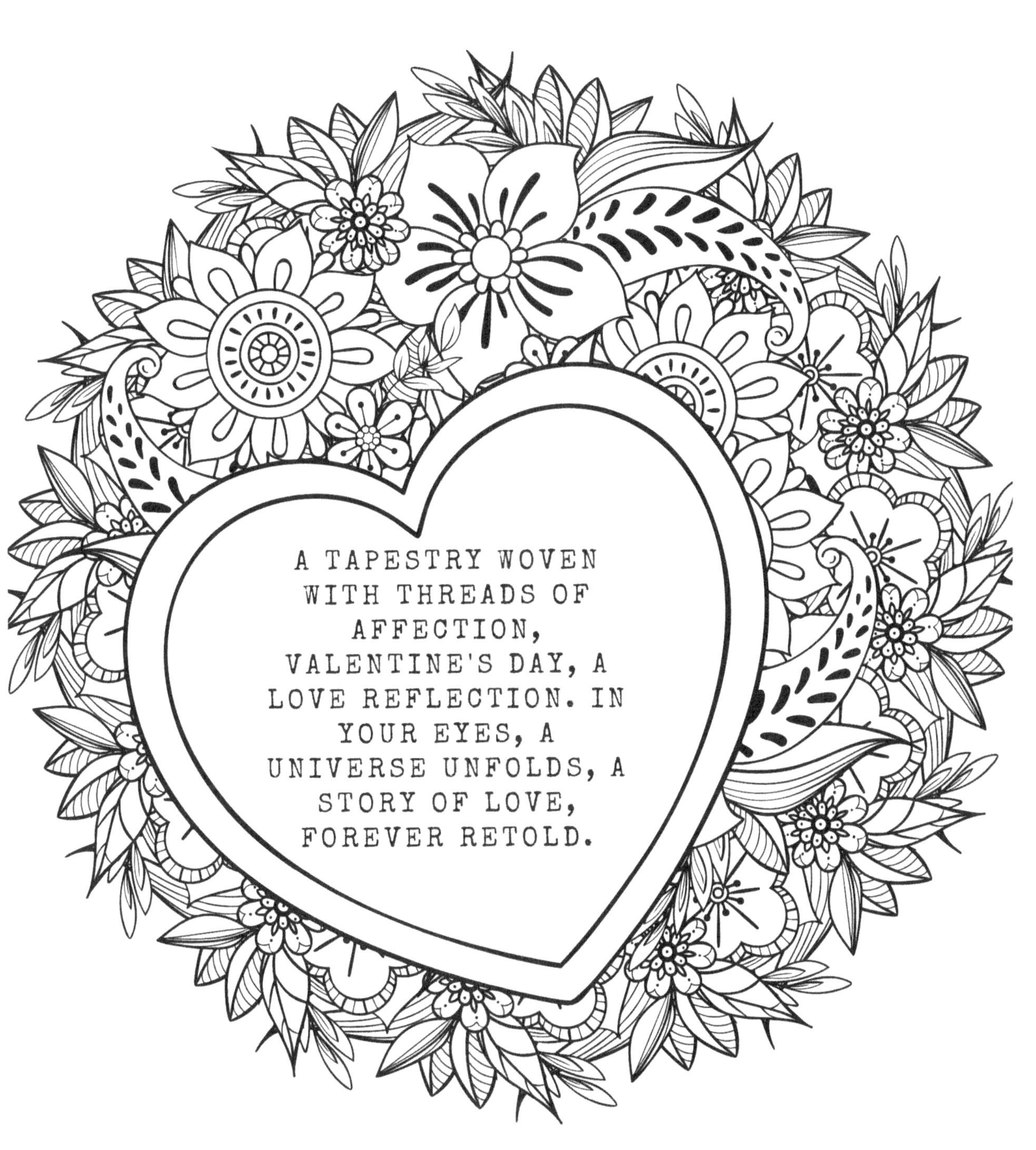
A TAPESTRY WOVEN
WITH THREADS OF
AFFECTION,
VALENTINE'S DAY, A
LOVE REFLECTION. IN
YOUR EYES, A
UNIVERSE UNFOLDS, A
STORY OF LOVE,
FOREVER RETOLD.

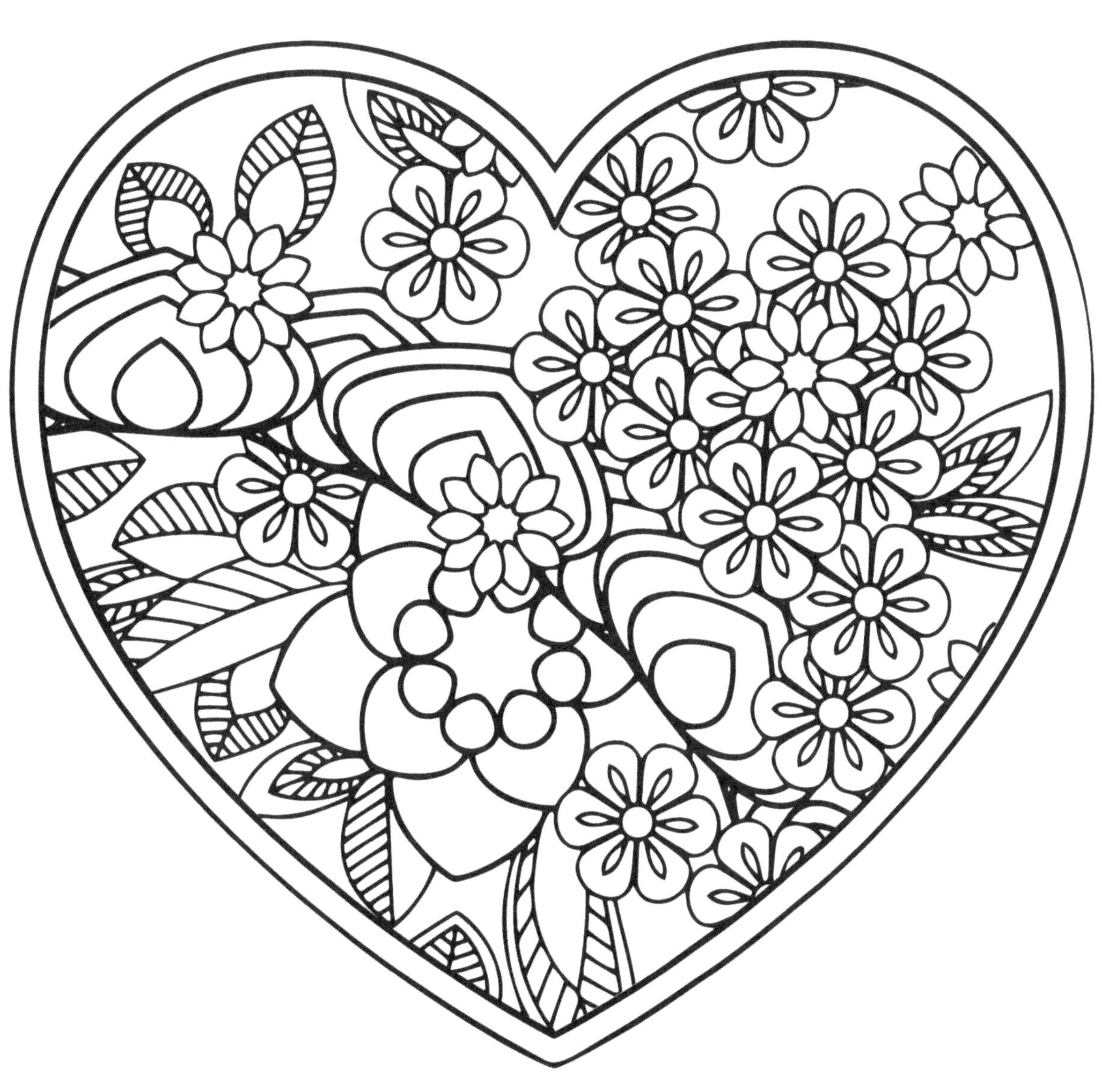

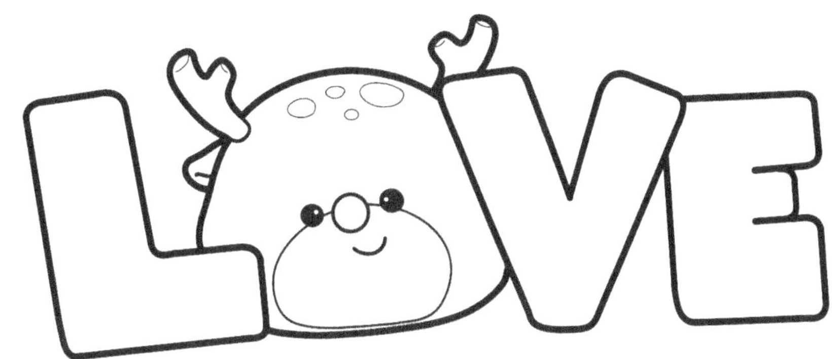

# LOVE

IN THE TWILIGHT'S TENDER EMBRACE, LOVE'S SONNET WEAVES, A SYMPHONY OF PASSION, WHERE THE HEART BELIEVES. BENEATH THE CANVAS OF CELESTIAL ART, OUR LOVE, A MASTERPIECE, AN ETERNAL CHART.WITH EVERY GAZE, A VERSE UNFOLDS, IN THE POETRY OF US, A STORY BOLDLY TOLD. MOONLIT WHISPERS, SECRETS SHARED, A DANCE OF SOULS, TWO HEARTS PAIRED.

IN THE GALLERY OF TIME, OUR LOVE DISPLAYED, A TIMELESS PORTRAIT, NEVER TO FADE. WITH EVERY SUNRISE AND EACH NIGHTFALL, OUR LOVE, A POETIC ECHO, ENCHANTING ALL.SO LET THE STARS COMPOSE OUR RHYME, IN THE BOUNDLESS PAGES OF LOVE'S PARADIGM. FOR IN THIS SONNET OF ETERNAL GRACE, OUR LOVE, A MASTERPIECE, IN LIFE'S EMBRACE.

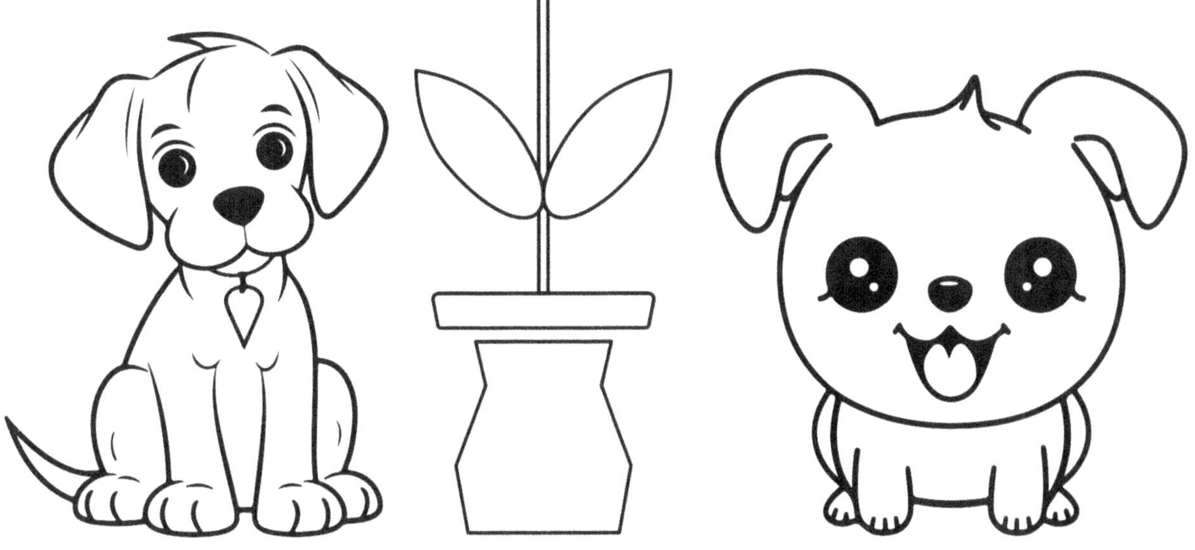